La Douleur Exquise

Poetry and Prose

Written by

LiAna Maria Rivera

Dedicated to the love that remains.

La Douleur Exquise.

Literally translated from French: The Exquisite Pain.

Being in love with someone you can't have;

unrequited love.

Poetry

La Douleur Exquise

D r u n k

*I'm drunk on your love
My appetite is gone.
All my body wants is you.*

*You've made me dizzy
I'm high on your eyes
The blood in my veins has
turned to wine
Happiness is impossible
Without you by my side.*

*I can't speak,
I'm giddy as fuck
You make me smile for no
reason at all.*

*I'm drunk on love
Incapable of thought
This is the best I can do.*

LiAna Maria Rivera

Love-struck,
Moonstruck,
No longer depressed.
High on your drugs,
Drunk on your love,
Totally obsessed
With you.

La Douleur Exquise

Alive

*I tried to love others that
came after you
But I've proven to be
incapable of that.
Now, you're back
And I can't imagine myself
with anyone else,
Nor do I want to.
The only one who holds my
full heart is you.
My soul, my mind, my body is
yours.
Nurture me, protect me;
Hurt me, destroy me;
That's all your choice.*

*You've broken my heart once
or twice,*

LiAna Maria Rivera

*You can break it a thousand
times.
This love will remain
Pure; always.*

*My trust— all I thought was
gone
Is still alive for you.
My love— all I wished was
gone
Has come alive in you.*

La Douleur Exquise

Locks and Keys
(part 2)

He put the first lock on my heart,
He's the only one who could break through all of them.
Another I loved gave me a hood, he tried.
Another I tainted by that ugly word that means nothing.
I melted the key;
Sealed my heart away somewhere not even I could reach.
But he knew everything.
I'm naked to him; I've always been.
I'll never be free; not from him.

LiAna Maria Rivera

I prayed he'd keep me locked away
In our perfect little world,
Isolated from everything else,
Isolated from everyone else.
To protect my heart and heal my body.
Only he can do that.
Only he has such power over me.
The only one I've ever wanted.
I'll do anything he asks of me,
I'll give him everything.
Because only he knows how to love me.
I'm completely, wholeheartedly devoted to him.

La Douleur Exquise

LiAna Maria Rivera

La Douleur Exquise

Nine Years

*For nine years of my life,
My love for you lay stagnant.
I swept it away to the back of my mind
And that's where I kept it.*

*Unbeknownst to me,
Though I knew it all along,
It remained;
Fermenting in my mind
Like a shelf of wine.*

*For nine long years,
My love for you lay stagnant
We both moved on.
I tried to love anyone else,
So long as they weren't you.
You loved others too,*

LiAna Maria Rivera

*But none of them loved you
quite like I do.*

*Nine years passed,
I ignored the love I had for
you
Even when I felt there was no
way out.
I cried all the time, I wanted
to die;
The pain, the sadness filled
my eyes,
Yet somehow you managed to
fill my heart.*

*Nine years passed since
we've seen each other
Yet the love I have has
blossomed.*

La Douleur Exquise

*My heart's abound with roses
and crystals;
My eyes covered in your
mystical veil;
Everything I see is beautiful
now.*

*Nine years passed, we've
both grown up.
I want you,
I love you
So much more than before.
For nine years of my life I
always have
And I might never stop.*

LiAna Maria Rivera

La Douleur Exquise

Still, You Loved Me

I know you can love me
How it was always meant to
be
You know the darkest parts of
me
You say I'm beautiful, despite
how ugly I can be
You know my personality, I'm
clingy, and irritating;
And still, you loved me.

I drove you away once before
You were afraid of me
But at my lowest, you saved
me
Then and now.
I remember when you ran
from me

LiAna Maria Rivera

And when you came back to me.

*You know the darkest parts of me,
You tell me I'm beautiful,
despite how ugly I can be
You know my personality, I'm clingy, and irritating;
And still, you loved me.
I never could've dreamed of this,
Because it hurt so much to dream before
I slept with thoughts of suicide
Without you there to hold me tight.
Your love healed my broken soul.*

La Douleur Exquise

You know the darkest parts of me,
You tell me I'm beautiful, despite how ugly I can be
You know my personality, I'm clingy, and irritating;
And still… you loved me.

LiAna Maria Rivera

La Douleur Exquise

My Vow

*I will love you
unapologetically
I'll never stop reminding you
every single day
Even if I don't say it, I will
show it
In a million different ways.
This love for you is the purest
emotion
I've ever felt before
You're the only one for me,
The only one I'll ever need.
I promise and vow from now
until I die,
I will love you
unapologetically;
I'll never stop reminding you
every single day.*

LiAna Maria Rivera

*Even if I don't say it, I will
show my love to you
In a million different ways.*

La Douleur Exquise

Yours

I love you more than you
could ever know
Even after everything that
happened before.
But none of that matters
anymore
Because you're mine
And I am yours
Now 'til forevermore.

LiAna Maria Rivera

La Douleur Exquise

Made For You

My body was made for you
My hair was made for your fingers
To comb through when you kiss me.
My lips were made for you.
To kiss yours, and everywhere else on your body.
My breasts were made for you.
A place to rest your heavy head.
My legs were made for you.
To wrap around your waist and pull you closer.
My arms were made for the same reason,

LiAna Maria Rivera

To keep you close to me.
The flower waiting where my
thighs meet
That was made for you too;
Dedicated to you.
My eyes were made to gaze
into yours,
My lashes to sing you a
lullaby of butterfly kisses.
My nose was made to breathe
your air.
My ears were made to hear
your voice.
My voice was made to say
your name.
My body was made for yours.
I fell in love with you,
And that's when I knew
This body was no longer my
own.

La Douleur Exquise

LiAna Maria Rivera

La Douleur Exquise

Butterfly Kisses

My sad brown eyes sing for him,
A sweet lullaby of butterfly kisses
And batting lashes
Make me cry, make me cry.

My sad brown eyes cry for him
The love I never knew.
His sad brown eyes, I saw it then
Even now they still seem alike
Despite what he says.
Even now they still shine
Despite all he's seen.

LiAna Maria Rivera

So, my sad brown eyes will sing for him
A sweet lullaby of butterfly kisses
My batting lashes
Vague and slightly familiar
From a past he couldn't forget.
All that happened to him;
Innocence—gone away,
Abandoned in the dust,
Fallen into my eyes,
Filling my mind
With memories once forgotten.

My sad brown eyes sing for him,
A sweet lullaby of butterfly kisses

La Douleur Exquise

And batting lashes
Make me cry, make me cry.
Apart we mourn a life
together
Unbeknownst to the other.

My sad brown eyes will sing
for him,
A sweet lullaby of butterfly
kisses
These batting lashes
Make me cry, make me cry.

I loved him then;
I still love him now;
And I'll love him until the day
I die.

Prose

La Douleur Exquise

LiAna Maria Rivera

Real.

When the first guy who ever broke your heart comes back to you better than he was before and a completely changed person, it pretty much negates all the assholes you had to deal with that came after him. My heart feels refreshed, like it's never been broken before. My insecurities don't exist anymore, my depression has reduced by immense proportion, and my anxiety is virtually dead because of him. I don't have to censor myself or hide what I'm really thinking. I can be completely real with him. He's the only one who has

La Douleur Exquise

this power over me, and to be honest, I wouldn't want it any other way.

LiAna Maria Rivera

Rainy Days.

On rainy days like today, I wish I could snuggle up with him and watch tv, hearing his heartbeat against my cheek, subtle caresses and chaste kisses. The only noise around us being the falling rain against the window, the low sound of the tv as we watch a show that we've both seen before, but never together; and the soft breathing between us.

La Douleur Exquise

Prisoner.

He still has my heart. He always has and always will, but I won't wait for him anymore. I'll give my body to whoever I want in the moment. I'll say I love whoever I want in the moment, but he and I will always know the truth.

I can't purely love anyone else with my entire heart but him, it's just impossible. The stories in my mind were born because of him. I write because of him. He was the start of everything. He's been my reason for living since I met him. It's stupid, it's probably even sick, but in this moment, it's exactly how I feel.

Even if he's not mine, I will always be his.

I will never be free of him. I don't want to be free of him.

If I had my way, I'd remain a prisoner of our perfect world in my own heart forever.

But I can't.

I vow from today until I die, I will work towards becoming someone he can be proud of. Someone I can be proud of. Someone who can support herself and make her own way and be completely independent. I will not be a burden to my family or myself

La Douleur Exquise

anymore. I may stumble along the way, things may happen, but I will become that nearly perfect person for myself.

It's my will.

LiAna Maria Rivera

How?

How do you get over a breakup when neither of you did anything wrong? It's always so easy to say, "This is why it didn't work out." but in our case, it's just so fucking messy. I know I have to let it go and move on, but that's so hard to do when I can't even hate him or when he can't hate me. The love is still there between us and there's always been something there even though we both ignored it for the longest time. This breakup isn't like the others... it doesn't even feel over despite the closure I'm pretending to have. It didn't feel like an

La Douleur Exquise

indefinite end. It feels more like a "See you later." or a "We'll be together one day, just not now." and I don't know how to move on from that. Just keep taking it day by day, I guess...

Is the universe testing us right now? Or were we simply not meant for each other?

I don't fucking know anymore.

LiAna Maria Rivera

Mi Principe.

He doesn't even feel like an ex and I refuse to call him that. He's still my friend because I can't let him go completely. knowing him, he can't let me go completely either. He's not friends with any of his exes no matter how petty their relationships ended and I'm not friends with any of mine either. Even if we're not together, he will always be in my life somehow, and I will always be in his. He's not my ex, he's my friend, my soulmate, and he'll always be my prince.

La Douleur Exquise

LiAna Maria Rivera

If We Ever Meet Again...

If we ever meet again, I don't know that I'd be able to hide my feelings from him. Time will heal us both enough to talk again, but that electricity... I don't think I'd be able to resist his current. this pull we have between us that draws me to him and him to me. If we ever meet again, I don't know that either of us could contain it. I don't know that either of us can even do that with a clear conscience. To want someone so much, but to not have them is dangerous.

Perhaps it's better we never meet again, because I

La Douleur Exquise

couldn't fathom thinking what I'm thinking now, just thinking about it.... the thought that I wouldn't feel guilty if it were him. We shouldn't meet again, because it's wrong. We shouldn't meet again, because these unresolved feelings need to remain suppressed. We shouldn't meet again, because all I need is to see his smile; all I need is to hear his voice; all I need is to hold his body close to mine, closer than he's ever been before.

We need to meet again, because this gravitational pull is too strong.

LiAna Maria Rivera

It's something beautiful.

Something selfish.

Something sinful, but between us, it's raw, it's pure, it's perfect. We won't meet again because we have to, we will meet again because we want to, we fucking want to more than anything.

La Douleur Exquise

Sinfully Pure.

I can't contain myself around him, he makes me want to be weak, only for him. Vulnerable, only for him. Simultaneously submissive and dominant, only for him. It can't be contained in these pages or words. It's more than desire, more than love, more than physical attraction.

His absence makes it easier to ignore, but not for long. I want more than his body, I want him to find home inside me, deep where no one else shall go. It feels impossible now, but I want him to be completely mine. Selfish, I

LiAna Maria Rivera

know, but it can't be helped. What I want from him is real, and what he wants from me is real. One way or another, we always get what we want. Though these feelings may be buried, ignored, neglected for years, they will grow and keep growing and growing and growing unbeknownst to both of us. When we meet again, we'll explode. I'll crash into him like waves on rocks, he'll erupt into me with the fiery passion of a thousand volcanoes. He'll love me in a way he can't love anyone else, because no one could make him feel this way except me; something deeper than his soul, deeper

La Douleur Exquise

*than his bones, deeper than
the sea and ground that
separates us. It's bad.
Reckless. Wrong. Beautiful.
Perfect. Right. It's sinfully
pure.*

LiAna Maria Rivera

La Douleur Exquise

October.

*October's end kisses the
angel devoid of wings,
leaving bruises behind on her
broken vessel. A reminder
that what is gentle can
always be deadly, and what is
loved can always be lost.*

LiAna Maria Rivera

In a Sea of Black Hair…

In a sea of black hair, I will always find you. I can see past the physical reality. I can see your aura; I can feel the pull of our string that connects you to me. All I need is to close my eyes and move my feet, and I will see you when I decide to open them again. In a sea of black hair, you will always find me. You know the color of my heart, the sound of my laugh, the wispy curl always out of place on my head. In a sea of black hair, we will always find each other. Because we can't stay apart forever, when the Universe wants

La Douleur Exquise

*more than anything for us to
be together.*

LiAna Maria Rivera

La Douleur Exquise

Consequences.

You never would've guessed in your wildest dreams that a girl that's the embodiment of everything you've ever wanted would be placed right in front of you. I forgive your younger self, because we were all young once. That girl you met on the last day of school, a girl who looked like a dream, but a total nerd the second she opened her mouth. A girl who once she met you felt something deep inside her. She didn't know how to explain it, nor how to deal with that constant nagging in her head all summer long. It was a simple touch against my waist. A

*place no boy touched on me
until you. It was a simple
word I'd heard so many times
before but coming from you it
sounded different. Other
people played the game at the
same time we did, but
between you and I, it felt like
more than just innocent
middle-schoolers celebrating
summer break. I wonder if
you and I were to play it
again... if it would feel
different this time around.*

*It would start as it did when
we were young, innocent. Old
friends meeting again for the
first time in a long time. A
simple ZAP! Followed by a
jolt of electricity straight into
your side. A kind of*

La Douleur Exquise

electricity that can't be replicated by any other friend, person, or lover. Recognition in our eyes. The realization that the person you're supposed to be with is right in front of you. The realization that you can't let her go again. She loves you, and you know it. You love her, and she knows it. The realization that neither of you can be together for reasons out of your control. Both of you did things that made it nearly impossible before you even had a chance. Both of you couldn't wait for the other. She for you to realize your own feelings, you for her to give you all the love

*she had been saving for you.
Such unfortunate
circumstances, but the Divine
loves to throw a wrench in
your plans when you least
expect it. Maintaining the eye
contact as these thoughts
and more flood your mind.
Until you see it in her eyes.*

*The longing, the yearning,
the strange mix of love and
lust for you in her eyes. She
makes you feel young again.
She makes you want to be
reckless. She makes you want
to give in to all your desires.
If just for a moment, you
could forget the world.
Forget everything around
you. Focus on nothing but
her. If you could both hold*

La Douleur Exquise

each other closer than you've ever been before, closer than you'd let anyone else. If her body could find a home in your arms, and your soul find home in her heart. To be in a place where your minds think as one, in perfect synchronization.

If we could be as one for a single moment, you know it would make me the happiest girl in the world. If you could reserve all your love for me and me alone for just one moment, I will never make you regret it. For this one moment, you'll belong to me and I'll belong to you.

LiAna Maria Rivera

Until daylight breaks in the horizon. It blinds you awake, and you turn to see her staring back at you. The tears in her eyes that she tries so desperately to hold back, but she can't hide anything from you. So, you hold her. You tell her you love her and always will, and your love alone is enough to satisfy her. Your love alone has always been enough to satisfy her. No more words are necessary. Finding comfort in the silence, gentle breathing, holding each other close for as long as possible, because neither of you know when you will again. She pulls away, knowing she must be the one

La Douleur Exquise

to do it. To disappear into another room so she wouldn't have to see you leave. You get dressed and walk to the door. Your hand shaking as you reach for the knob. You ponder only for a moment about the time you were kids. Innocently playing a silly game. Meeting on the last day of school. Not fully knowing why the connection was so strong back then, and it's only as you could barely hear her breaking down in tears in the other room that you understand.

These are the consequences of meeting your soulmate too soon and realizing it far too late.

LiAna Maria Rivera

La Douleur Exquise

Selfishly and Selflessly.

You need to say it, to say the right words for her to move on, for her to heal after you. Deep down you know you should, deep down you know it would be easier for both of you. You want what's best for her, you want her to be happy even if that happiness can't include you. Though you say it's what you want, deep down; deeper than your love for her, you know she's yours. You don't want her to move on. You don't want her to be happy without you because you know she can't be. You don't want her to have a life without you in it, you don't want anyone else to touch her the way you used to, you don't want anyone else to find a home in her heart because her heart belongs to you and you alone. You can't say the words she needs to hear, because it isn't how you truly feel. You can't lie to her like you once did. you can't say "Goodbye.", you can't say "Farewell.", you can't say "It's over.", you can't say "I'm done with you.", you can't say "We're finished.", "We're through.", "I never want to see you again.", "Fuck off.", "Get out of my life.". You can't say these words because you still love her, even though there's no point. You still love her,

La Douleur Exquise

even though you've laid out a path for yourself, and you must stick to it. Try as you might to bury all these feelings, to sweep them under the rug, to ignore them for as long as you possibly can; you still love her. You still love her selfishly and selflessly. You can't say what she needs to hear. You can't say it; so, you don't.

LiAna Maria Rivera

A Future Dead to Us...

I'm so in love with you, it makes me sick. I can't eat because all my body wants is you, I can't sleep because when I close my eyes, you're there. You're always in my head. you shot my anxiety and insecurity dead, replacing it with an image of you. But I wouldn't want it any other way. If I had to dream of such exquisite pain, of an ideal love we once had that only exists now in my dreams, in my heart, I would take it over the anxiety, the fear, and the insecurity you killed in me. I don't wish to be rid of these dreams of you,

La Douleur Exquise

of us, of a future dead to us,
even if they drive me mad.

LiAna Maria Rivera

Crazy.

You always secretly liked my crazy side, though... didn't you? The silly girl whispering jokes to you every day at school. I scared you back then because you weren't used to it, and to be frank, I scared myself as well. You liked the attention I gave you, but it scared you at the same time. For some reason though, you always came back for more. might you come back to me now? Could I be so lucky as to think a dream may become reality once again? Or does this false hope for castles in the air make me every bit as crazy as I used to be?

La Douleur Exquise

Comfortable Distance.

You must have always loved me or cared about me or thought about me at random points in your life. Either that or you saw an easy target. Someone who would do anything and everything for you. It would be easier to think you only showed the slightest interest in me to pass the time, to have fun, to fill a temporary void. It would be better to believe that, but that's not the truth is it? It was always you. Every conversation always started with you. The moment we met, I asked everyone in the room a question and you answered it. I can't

*remember the question now.
It was probably irrelevant
anyway. Strangely enough
the only thing I do remember
from that day is we couldn't
stop talking to each other
once we started.*

*When I saw you again, I
could barely contain the
butterflies. We were so
innocent, so precious, and
what I thought was
friendship, I slowly realized
was something else. Between
us it felt different and I
couldn't understand why.
Our conversations weren't
memorable in the slightest,
but I know I annoyed you
sometimes with my blind
affection.*

La Douleur Exquise

If you had asked me back then why I liked you, I wouldn't have had an answer. There was no concrete reason. If you asked me now, it would be because you were easy to talk to, I felt comfortable with you, I felt at home looking into your eyes. And after you grew fed up with me, after you cut me out completely, I wanted nothing more than to die. my creativity and all my ideas blossomed from the first crack you etched on my heart, so I didn't end my life solely for that.

I ignored you for years. I pretended you didn't exist. Until you contacted me again, three years after you cut me out.

I had moved on, I found someone else, despite the incessant melancholia I felt with him, I finally had a life again that didn't revolve around you. So, I kept my guard up, because back then I had him. The hood I wore gave me strength; the strength I needed to keep you away.

I remembered everything you said before, and I didn't get too close. I ignored what my heart wanted. We became friends again, and both of us kept a comfortable distance. But there was always

La Douleur Exquise

something between us that we couldn't ignore for long. Five long years passed, though we spoke a little here and there, we both kept the guard up. It wasn't until my depression was at its worst to the point where I was contemplating suicide every day because I couldn't see past it. You saved me once again and fell in love with me in the process.

As adults, it felt deeper, it felt real, it wasn't innocent anymore, but somehow it was still just as pure as it's always been. You finally reciprocated my feelings without anyone telling you to, and it was bliss. Though you hadn't physically touched me since we were kids, your beautiful words felt stronger than any embrace.

Actions may speak louder than words, yet I still believed every word you said. Simply writing messages back and forth everyday was enough. Simply loving me was enough. Everything you did was enough. Though I would like more, I would love more, love is all I wanted and that's exactly what you gave me.

We've receded back into that comfortable distance. A place we've always been. A place where I can watch you and

La Douleur Exquise

admire you from far away, a place you can watch me and admire me from far away. A place where I can sense you, a place where you can sense me. A place where only we exist.

LiAna Maria Rivera

Empire.

All these years, all these pages, every word, every drop of my blood in ink spilled into my castle of parchment was because of you. It all started because of my love for you. I could make an empire out of all the love in my heart and I intend to. It's the only way I can prove my love to you now, the only way that's left.

La Douleur Exquise

Brand New.

My heart has taken quite a beating since you last saw it, and you repaired it to be brand new again like it was before you broke it. I couldn't love anyone more than you because you are my heart. Every beat in it belongs to you.

LiAna Maria Rivera

Stronger.

He loved me when my soul was weakest; battered, and almost broken. He remade me into someone stronger than I ever was before. For that, I am forever grateful.

La Douleur Exquise

Greed.

I'm greedier for his love more than grave robbers are for jewelry. His eyes dark and deep pulled me in, I want the golden light that shines from them. The light he can only show to me. The light in my own eyes only shine for him. Only he can make my eyes glisten with tears. Tears from heartbreak, tears from happiness, tears from ecstasy, tears from yearning, grieving from years of holding on too tight. He's greedy like me, but for something else entirely. For these tears. He's greedy to hurt me. His hatred for me is strong, feelings that he buried and could never embrace, only the moment he did, it got snatched away. Feelings darker than his eyes. Darker than my tears drenched in mascara from the long nights without him. He's greedy for my pain. And I'm greedy for his love. It's toxic, it's deadly, it's addicting. I'm greedy for more of him and all the things he makes me feel. No matter how much it hurts me.

La Douleur Exquise

LiAna Maria Rivera

Barely Remember.

My heart's in disrepair without his gentle touch. I barely remember what he felt like. Every moment together freezes in my mind, but I still can't remember. I barely remember how he held my hand once in the schoolyard, but somehow still remember every word he said to me that day. The most beautiful year of my adolescent life was spent with him and though I barely remember parts of it, I can't remember a time when I was ever happier.

La Douleur Exquise

Translucent.

He scares me, because he sees right through me. how I wish I could hide it all from him. That I can move on, but it's not possible. I'm stubborn, I will never be truly happy without him, because I haven't met anyone like him thus far. Anyone that makes me feel how he does. Why him? Why do I have to love him? And why must he see through every fake smile and every forced laugh? Why do I waste time with every mask I pull over my eyes in vain attempts to hide tears from someone who sees through me and all my layers like fucking glass? And like fucking glass I shatter into pieces. Only this time, he can't pick me up again. This time I am alone. I will fade from his memory for a second time. I have become nothing but a ghost to him. A translucent, invisible, nonexistent ghost of the past. But to me, he will remain in my past, my present, and my future.

La Douleur Exquise

Corrupted.

Temporary happiness is as fleeting as feathers fallen from angels who have lost their way. I am one of them. Love made me a lost cause. Love gave me thoughts of a sinner. To think the way I think. To live in a delusion brought about by pretty words and a beautiful smile. Those dreamy eyes like gold lit a fire in my heart and melted away the chains that kept me sane. I have a heart only for him. I am incapable of loving anyone else, but instead of telling, I keep it hidden. He cast a shadow in my heart. A permanent darkness like a tattoo, but it's invisible to those who cannot see past the mask. He was the first and last I loved. The one I loved as an angel, the one I love as a raven; twice fallen. This wound he cut open in me healed on the road to repentance, but somewhere along the way I took a wrong turn and now, it's opened up again. The blood trails endlessly because my love for him is endless. He's corrupted me once again, he's tainted me with deception once again, he's made me slip into despair once again. Only this time, I believe, he may have loved me back.

La Douleur Exquise

The Coven.

My house is a coven of witches; witches of which know not the comfort of men, for when we get even a glimpse of it, the vague phantom of love, a force unbeknownst to us snatches it away from the grasp of our hand.

So, you ask the question of which: a witch like me has ever left love? Yes; I've felt it, real; I've felt it passionately; strange and benevolent or at least it used to be, but has a witch like me felt true love? Completely, not at all, only barely; only when the very thought of it

*bounces around from one
side of my sick skull to the
other. That which a witch like
me has felt such a malevolent
emotion of that unrequited,
unrelenting, unforgiving
phantom; something beautiful
that could have been, but
something never realized.
For the only love of which a
witch like me has ever known
is a love known too late.*

*The coven of witches in
which I reside is one made up
of women who know not the
love of men.*

*For every man we know we
could have loved, is a man
we should have loved back
then.*

La Douleur Exquise

Second Thoughts.

Parts of me wished he'd leave what happened between us in the past. By ignoring me and my attempts at friendship, it shows me that he must still be hurting. Either that or he's too busy or he's ignoring the pain and everything having to do with me because he doesn't want to hurt me more than he already has or he feels like he needs to stay away from me because of the situation he's in. Maybe he doesn't trust himself or maybe he resents me for giving up on him so easily. For not being that headstrong love-obsessed girl that he used to know all those years ago. The girl I used to be who changed because of him. Instead of him breaking my heart, I broke his. With many words left unsaid, endless scenarios that could've played out, I chose the words that pulled us apart. I thought if it didn't come from me, it would've come from him or maybe he could've said some kind of pretty words to make me believe in something that was impossible. Maybe I could've tried harder, maybe I could've spoken with my heart and made a complete fool of myself. Every fiber in my body screaming out to say what I was really thinking:

La Douleur Exquise

"So, you made a mistake, no one's perfect. I love you anyway."

"I'll stay by your side no matter what."

"We can make it work."

"I don't care about that. I will support you and I want to be with you."

"I'll do anything for you, I love you."

"I trust you and I want you."

"Don't give up on our love."

"Well... then give me a baby too."

With so many things in my mind, I was in shock. so

instead I chose to say goodbye. Because nothing else made sense at the time. While all those thoughts were in my mind, the darker, smarter, truer thoughts were louder:

"Why would he want you when he could have her?"

"She's closer to him in ways you never have been, and never will be."

"Of course, he'd choose her over you, she's carrying his baby."

"What makes you think he would want you at all after that?"

La Douleur Exquise

"He's been silent for almost three days now; he's already given up on you."

"Give up and end it now; there's no point."

I was afraid of him leaving, so I left first. I was afraid of him choosing her over me, so I took away his choice and made my own. The pride I worked years to build finally won over my heart, so that's why I didn't try.

But there's still a part of me that wonders... what if? If rejection was inevitable, why didn't I try the other option? Why didn't I let him break my heart again? Why didn't I say what I was really feeling?

LiAna Maria Rivera

Why did I take the easy way out? Did that make him think I didn't love him after all? Despite everything I said and everything we spoke about; does he think I lied? Does he hate me for that? I still love him now, so what was the point of leaving him when he probably needed me the most?

But the biggest question that lingers in my mind from that day to even now was...

"Do you still love me?"

I didn't ask because I was afraid of his answer. that he would be honest and say, "No." or fill me with empty hopes and say, "I can't."

La Douleur Exquise

That everything he said was a lie. That he didn't really feel what said he felt for me.

The fear I thought was gone came back, but in a different way entirely. I've changed since middle school, expecting disappointment all the time that I didn't give him a fair chance. That's something I have to live with, and I will.

I will live happily.

LiAna Maria Rivera

La Douleur Exquise

I Will.

How wrong have I been until now? Writing these words from a fungus that spread in my heart and decayed me from the inside out? How could I have been so idiotic to think the reason I exist now is because of him?

No… he did nothing to aid in my happiness.

He did nothing to aid in my happiness.

He did nothing.

These words are mine.

These stories are mine.

These poems, the prose, every single world dripping from

LiAna Maria Rivera

my hands and heart and brain and eyes.

They're all mine.

This exquisite pain is mine.

The feeling of being left behind.

The feeling of being shot dead.

The feeling of being taken for granted

Over and over and over again.

They're all mine.

I have my words,

I have my heart,

I have my mind,

La Douleur Exquise

I have my hands,

I have my body.

This body is mine.

Never his.

This body belongs to me.

No one else.

I don't need him, because he only holds me back.

I don't need his love, I'm better off without it.

I'm happier without him.

I'll never see him again, because I don't want to.

He can drown in that a sea of black hair forever,

LiAna Maria Rivera

*I will never look for him
again.*

*He didn't write these stories,
he only served me with pain.*

*I never contemplated suicide
before he came into my life.*

I will never turn back again.

*Walk ahead, stand up
straight, write beautiful
words until the end.*

*Walk ahead, stand up
straight, write beautiful
words until the end.*

*Walk ahead, stand up
straight, write beautiful
words until the end.*

La Douleur Exquise

I will.

LiAna Maria Rivera

Thank God.

All I've done means nothing. Thank God I didn't sacrifice more than my time, energy, and love. Thank God the things I sacrificed don't really exist. Thank God love from a man isn't real.

La Douleur Exquise

Solitude Over Companionship.

I feel more at peace with myself than any lover could ever give me. Those who disagree, find me someone that would never leave, someone that would love me, and put me before everything. Find me a lover that would want me and obsess over the way I laugh and make fun of my nervous ticks but still give me space when I need it. One that would give the same amount of love I give. One that would keep giving and keep reciprocating. One that would dedicate energy and time and love and intimacy and show me everything that makes life worth living, one that would dedicate themselves to me, to my happiness. Find me someone whom I could love, someone beautiful like me, inside and out. One who can give me everything I want. One that can give me what all the others before never could. Find me someone who could love me above everything else and not make half-hearted promises and say pretty words to make me believe them. Only then would I want to be in love again. Only then would I prefer companionship over solitude.

La Douleur Exquise

LiAna Maria Rivera

Ideas.

Put ideas in my head and watch them blossom into works of art. Again, I am left alone to mourn a life without you, to return to that dark corner in my mind where your memory haunts my skull and reminds me every single day that ideas were all they were. A storm started in my brain, bringing about calm and rain and gentle wind until tornadoes formed and hurricanes crashed into every dream we created, and the wretched storm of our life together ended with the last line of our love song.

La Douleur Exquise

So, go on. Put ideas into my head. make me fall in love with you. I welcome it now more than ever before. Let me turn my grief into something beautiful, because my hands and my mind and my words are always left behind every single time you decide to leave.

LiAna Maria Rivera

Goddess.

Love is temporary. Love doesn't exist. Love isn't real. Love is just as real as fiction. I suppose that's why I love writing. because I can make people love the way I want to be loved. I can make people do anything I want them to. I control their lives as a goddess of ink and parchment. I write the love I wish to receive. I write the love I know I will never get, because that kind of love only exists in fiction. It only exists between the lines. It only exists in these pages. It only exists in my mind. In this ill mind of mine, love is beautiful. In this ill mind of

La Douleur Exquise

*mine, love is real. In this ill
mind of mine, love still exists.*

La Douleur Exquise: Poetry and Prose copyright © 2019 by LiAna Maria Rivera. No part of this book may be used or reproduced in any manner without written permission except in the case of reprints in the context of reviews.

ISBN: 978-1-951417-02-4

Library of Congress Control Number: 2019919628

Cover Design by LiAna Maria Rivera

About the Author:

LiAna Maria Rivera is an artist of various mediums namely: writing, drawing, and music.

Her purpose in life is to call the inner melancholy that lay dormant within her and transform it into something beautiful in any creative way her mind wills it.

Her writing and art styles are heavily inspired by the romantic era of art and literature. As expected, she loves writing poetry, horror, and psychological thrillers. Despite this, she's a softie for beautiful love stories and likes to incorporate themes of love into a vast majority of her work.

She loves animals, but no animal more than Mr. BooBooKitty Cuddles, a black and white seven-year young cat. Rainy, cloudy days spent cuddling with him and getting lost in a book are what happy times are made of for this strange lady.

When she's not cooing over how adorable her cat is, she's probably writing a blog post about how the decomposition process makes flowers shine brighter than the Supermoon.

www.ingramcontent.com/pod-product-compliance
Lightning Source LLC
Chambersburg PA
CBHW030122100526
44591CB00009B/490